LITTLE GOLDEN

Picture Dictionary

BY DIANE MULDROW
ILLUSTRATED BY BOB STAAKE

🏆 A GOLDEN BOOK • NEW YORK

Copyright © 2002 by Random House, Inc. All rights reserved under Intenational and Pan-American Copyright Conventions. Published in the United States by Golden Books, an imprint of Random House Children's Books, a division of Random House, Inc., New York, and simultaneously in Canada by Random House of Canada Limited, Toronto. Originally published by Golden Books, an imprint of Random House Children's Books, a division of Random House, Inc. in 2002. Golden Books, A Golden Book, A Little Golden Book, the G colophon, and the distinctive gold spine are registered trademarks of Random House, Inc.
Library of Congress Control Number: 2001096563
ISBN: 0-307-96035-8
www.goldenbooks.com
Printed in the United States of America 20 19 18 17 16 15 14

A a

acorn

The **acorn** is the nut that falls from the oak tree.

airplane

The **airplane** flies up high in the sky.

alligator

This **alligator** lives in the swamp. It has sharp teeth!

apple

My **apple** is shiny and red.

apron

The chef wears an **apron** to keep his clothes clean.

balloon

My **balloon** is full of air.

B b

bear

The furry **bear** lives in the mountains.

bicycle

I can't wait to ride my new **bicycle**.

book

My dad is reading a **book** about birds.

butterfly

The **butterfly** has colorful wings.

car

Let's go for a ride in the **car**.

castle

A **castle** is a home for a king and queen.

clock

The **clock** tells us what time it is.

clown

A **clown** makes people laugh.

computer

Grandpa is typing a letter on his **computer**.

daisy

The **daisy** is a pretty wildflower.

D d

dance

Krissie likes to **dance** to the music.

dog

My **dog** is chewing on his bone.

doll

My **doll** can close her eyes.

duck

A **duck** is a bird that likes to swim.

E e

ears

I hear with my **ears**.

egg

Crack!
A chick is hatching
from its **egg**!

elephant

The **elephant**
has a long nose
called a trunk.

envelope

Ben is putting a letter
in an **envelope**. Now
he can mail his letter.

eyes

I see with my **eyes**.

fish

Fish live underwater.

flower

I grew this **flower** in my garden.

fork

Lorrie eats spaghetti with a **fork**.

fox

The **fox** has a bushy tail.

frog

This **frog** lives at the pond.

giraffe

The **giraffe** has a long neck that helps it reach tasty leaves.

goat

My **goat** has horns and eats grass.

grapes

Grapes are sweet and juicy.

guitar

Joshua can play the **guitar** and sing.

gymnast

The **gymnast** jumps off the balance beam.

hat

Grandma is wearing her favorite **hat**.

H
h

hen

My **hen** is the mother of these little chicks.

hop

I can **hop** on one foot!

horse

The **horse** gallops through the field.

house

I live in a red brick **house**.

I i

ice-cream cone

It's nice to eat an **ice-cream cone** on a hot summer day.

icicle

When dripping water freezes, an **icicle** is formed.

igloo

An **igloo** is a house made of ice or snow.

iron

A hot **iron** smooths away wrinkles.

J j

jacket

Molly's **jacket** keeps her warm.

jack-o'-lantern

We carved my **jack-o'-lantern** out of a pumpkin.

jar

The pickles are in a **jar**.

jelly

Sam puts grape **jelly** on his toast.

joey

A baby kangaroo is called a **joey**.

kayak

Jane is paddling her **kayak** on the river.

kettle

Soup is cooking in the **kettle**.

key

A **key** unlocks a door.

kite

It's fun to fly a **kite** on a windy day.

kitten

A **kitten** is a young cat.

ladder

The house painter uses a **ladder**.

lamb

A **lamb** is a baby sheep.

leaf

The **leaf** fell off the tree.

lemon

A **lemon** is a fruit with a sour taste.

lion

The **lion** is a big wild cat.

merry-go-round

The **merry-go-round** goes around and around.

mittens

Roberta's **mittens** keep her hands warm.

monkey

The **monkey** can swing from tree to tree.

moon

The **moon** shines in the sky at night.

mouse

The **mouse** has whiskers and a long tail.

N n

nest

The bluebirds live in a **nest**.

newspaper

Mom reads the **newspaper** for news from all over the world.

nose

Hayley smells the cookies with her **nose**.

nurse

A **nurse** helps care for sick people.

nut

A **nut** has a hard shell.

ocean

The ship is sailing on the wide blue **ocean**.

octopus

The **octopus** has eight arms. It lives in the ocean.

orange

The **orange** is a sweet fruit. It grows on a tree.

oven

Yum! I can smell the turkey roasting in the **oven**.

owl

"Whooo!" cries the **owl**. It hunts at night.

P p

pajamas

Ashley likes to sleep in her pink **pajamas**.

parrot

The **parrot** is a colorful bird that can talk.

pie

Who ate a piece of the cherry **pie**?

pony

The gentle **pony** is smaller than a horse.

potato

A **potato** is a vegetable that grows under the ground.

queen

A **queen** is the ruler of her country. She wears a crown.

Q q

quilt

Mom sewed my **quilt** from scraps of fabric.

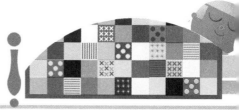

rabbit

The **rabbit** has soft fur and a fluffy tail.

rainbow

After a rainstorm, a **rainbow** may appear when the sun comes out.

ring

My sister wears a **ring** on her finger.

rocket

The **rocket** is flying up to the moon!

rose

The **rose** is my favorite flower.

sled

Whee! Kathy slides down the hill on her **sled**.

snowman

We built a **snowman** on a cold, snowy day.

spider

The **spider** wants to catch a fly in its web.

squirrel

The **squirrel** lives in a tree. It is eating an acorn.

suitcase

I'm going on a trip.
I packed my clothes
in a **suitcase**.

telephone

I like to talk to my grandma
on the **telephone**.

toothbrush

I brush my teeth with my
toothbrush every day.

train

"Whoo-whoo!"
The **train** is chugging
down the track.

truck

This **truck**
can carry a big load.

turtle

The **turtle** can hide in its shell.

umbrella

Lauren's **umbrella** keeps her dry in the rain.

underwear

We wear **underwear** under our clothes.

valentine

Jack gave me a **valentine**. It says "Be Mine."

vest

Grandpa dresses up in his red **vest**.

violet

The **violet** is a flower
that can live in the **shade**.

violin

Louisa plays pretty music
on her **violin**.

volleyball

It's fun to play
volleyball on
the beach.

W
W

wagon

My little sister likes
to ride in the **wagon**.

wash

I help **wash**
the car.

watermelon

The **watermelon** is sweet and good to eat. It grows on the ground.

whale

A grown-up **whale** is huge. This one has come up for air!

window

The cat is looking out the **window**.

X ray

The doctor took an **X ray** of my arm. She can see the bones that way.

X
X

yak

The **yak** has long hair that keeps it warm.

Y
Y

yarn

Aunt Clara is knitting a sweater with green **yarn**.

yo-yo

Dan can do tricks with his **yo-yo**.

zebra

The **zebra** has black and white stripes.

zipper

Laura's jacket stays closed with a **zipper**.

zoo

We visit the animals at the **zoo**.